MEE MEE CHAI

The Stories in Paintings

Every painting has a story to tell

meemeechai.com

First published by meemeechai.com 2024

Copyright © 2024 by MEE MEE CHAI

All rights reserved. No part of this publication may be reproduced, stored or transmitted in any form or by any means, electronic, mechanical, photocopying, recording, scanning, or otherwise without written permission from the publisher. It is illegal to copy this book, post it to a website, or distribute it by any other means without permission.

MEE MEE CHAI asserts the moral right to be identified as the author of this work.

MEE MEE CHAI has no responsibility for the persistence or accuracy of URLs for external or third-party Internet Websites referred to in this publication and does not guarantee that any content on such Websites is, or will remain, accurate or appropriate.

First edition

Editing by Kate Simpson
Cover art by Mee Mee Chai

This book was professionally typeset on Reedsy.
Find out more at reedsy.com

DEDICATION

Thank you God for all the blessings you have bestowed upon me.
To my mum, for her unwavering support and belief in me, which continues to inspire me even though she is no longer with us.
To Kate, for generously volunteering her time to edit and proofread this book.
And to Max, for reigniting my dreams and guiding me through every leap with steadfast support and encouragement.
I will embrace the vast skies, white clouds, and endless horizons ahead with courage.

Contents

Foreword	ii
Introduction	1
A living rainbow	2
A walk in the field	4
Celebration	7
Connection	10
Green Paradise	13
In the Park	15
Journey Home	18
Midnight in Paris	21
Little Pond	24
Meet me at sunset	27
See You Again	30
The Sea and Me	33
Conclusion	36
Afterword	37

Foreword

My mother once harboured a dream of seeing me publish an art book that would captivate countless readers. Initially, I regarded this as mere fantasy, but her unwavering belief and actions gradually led me to reconsider. When she took up painting between 2018 and 2019, she infused her art with her own stories, each brushstroke a gentle reminder of her vision for the book. Her enthusiasm was infectious, and though I initially encouraged her to keep her focused, I soon found myself carried along by her dream.

To uplift her spirits and maintain her focus, I made a promise: if she completed ten paintings, I would organize a solo exhibition just for her. Despite battling severe heart disease and a brain tumour that left her frail and partially paralysed, she poured every ounce of her energy into her art. In just a few short months, she surpassed her goal, completing thirteen vibrant, rainbow-themed paintings — each one more beautiful than the last.

True to my word, I arranged a solo exhibition for her. The joy on her face as she saw her artwork displayed for friends and family was beyond words. At 83, she became a sensation, earning the affectionate nickname 'Rainbow Grandma' from the media. Her story touched the lives of many, not only inspiring admiration but also encouraging others, particularly those in their later years, to pursue their dreams despite the odds. Sadly, just two months after her triumphant exhibition, my mother passed away peacefully. Yet her legacy lives on in the hearts of those moved by her art and story.

From my earliest memories, my mother was a masterful storyteller. She had a gift for weaving tales that could captivate anyone, whether she was recounting a movie plot or inventing a story on the spot. We, her eager audience, would gather on the cool cement floor, hanging on her every word as her stories came to life. Her love for storytelling ignited within me a passion to write and draw, to create my own narratives inspired by my feelings, experiences, and the world around me. I became fascinated by the stories paintings could tell, the lives they could reflect.

In fulfilling my mother's dream, I now present this book — a collection of my paintings, each accompanied by its own story. This is more than an art book; it is a reflection of my life, my emotions, and my journey. Within these pages, you will find clouds, skies, seas, flowers, and musings that have shaped who I am. It is a journey I invite you to take with me, one that I hope brings you moments of light, surprise, and hope, just as my mother's story has brought to so many.

The Artist-Author
Mee Mee Chai

Introduction

Welcome to the world of my art. As you journey through the stories woven into each piece, you will find a reflection of my own path, including my thoughts, emotions, and the myriad experiences that have shaped who I am. It is often said that art mirrors life, and in this collection, you will discover how deeply my work is intertwined with my personal narrative.

I find that the quiet solitude of night, when the world outside is hushed and still, is when my creativity blooms most vividly. In these peaceful hours, as others rest, inspiration flows with unrestrained grace. I am drawn to acrylic paints for their fluidity and versatility, preferring them over oils, whose intense aroma can be overwhelming. Each artwork you encounter within these pages has been lovingly crafted with acrylics on canvas or wood.

The paintings are presented without a specific order, allowing each one to reveal its unique story at its own pace. I invite you to immerse yourself in them as you wish, exploring the collection according to your own rhythm and preference. It is my sincere hope that these works resonate with you, bringing a touch of beauty, reflection, and joy into your life.

A living rainbow

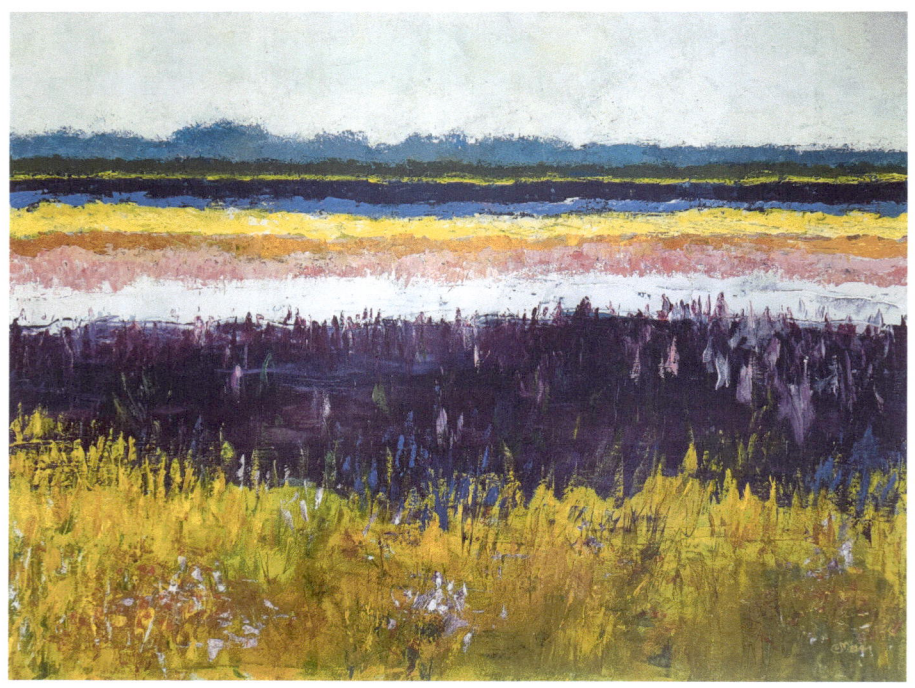

Acrylic on canvas 80x100cm

On December 8, 1941, when Japan invaded Malaya, a British colony, my mother was a primary school student. The upheaval of war forced her to abandon her education, leaving her studies unfinished. It was only after the conflict subsided that she had the opportunity to attend night classes and pursue her education further. She often reflected on a teacher's comforting words: "Good things come after bad times, just like seeing a colourful rainbow after it rains." Inspired by this sentiment, she frequently gazed at the sky, hoping to spot a rainbow.

There were moments when she would see twin rainbows arching together. Alongside her love for rainbows, my mother was captivated by the ever-shifting shapes of clouds. Her teacher had once said, "Clouds can look like anything," a concept she found enchanting, though not fully understood at the time. To her, clouds morphed into dogs, sheep, and even joyful faces, bringing her immense delight.

The sky, with its myriad forms, was a source of beauty and wonder for her.

I vividly recall the moment when, at 82, my mother picked up a paintbrush for the first time. Her debut piece was a painting of a rainbow. Despite her illness, she created thirteen paintings, each featuring a rainbow. I held a solo exhibition for her artwork, and it was the first time since my father's passing that I saw her face light up with genuine happiness.

She passed away peacefully in her sleep just two months later. Her life, filled with its share of trials and triumphs, was expressed through the vibrant rainbows she painted in her later years.

As I paint this bright field of flowers today, I envision it as a rainbow descending from the sky and touching the earth, a rainbow that will linger here for a while before it fades. This imagery represents the rainbow in each of our lives: bright, fleeting, and beautiful, urging us to live fully.

Reflecting on my mother's paintings, I see them as her rainbow, vividly imprinted on this land. I miss not only her artwork but also her radiant smile, the lines etched into her cheeks when she laughed, and the wrinkles on her nose from her joyful expressions.

I hope our lives can mirror this vast field of flowers: radiant and beautiful like a rainbow, continually growing and flourishing with each passing day, bringing joy, colour, and warmth to everyone around us, just as these blossoms do in nature.

A walk in the field

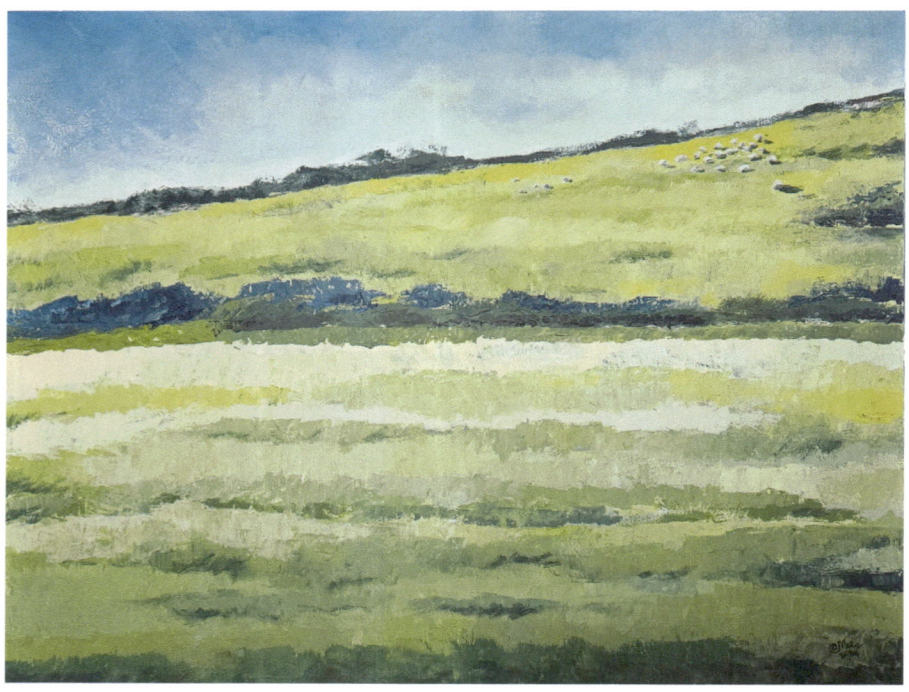

Acrylic on canvas 80x100cm

I often find solace in painting expansive fields dotted with cows and sheep that seem to emerge from fairytale scenes. Although my canvases can never capture the tangible scent of grass or the fragrant whispers of nature, they strive to convey its essence through the heart.

I recall a poignant afternoon last year when inspiration struck as I sat in my studio, envisioning a lush green field. This vision reminded me of a film from my childhood, There Is My Home, which we watched at the cinema on Children's Day with our form teacher. The film's depiction of a wooden house on the prairie captivated my young imagination. Motivated by these recollections, I painted a pastoral scene featuring a field and a flock of sheep, which later graced the "Elemental Art Exhibition" at Chelsea Gallery.

At the exhibition, several visitors expressed how my painting offered them a respite from their hectic urban lives. It seemed to serve as a breath of fresh air, encouraging them to slow down and savour nature's simple pleasures. Walking barefoot on these fields is a tactile delight; though the grass can be prickly, it feels like a gentle massage.

I often imagine myself residing in a quaint wooden house on a hillside, adorned in a floral cotton dress, tending to a garden of vegetables and flowers, and caring for an assortment of animals: chickens, ducks, sheep, dogs, and pigeons. Mornings would begin with me gathering a bouquet of roses from the garden to place in a glass vase on the breakfast bar. I would then set up my easel outside, capturing the surrounding beauty in my daily paintings. On days when I'm not painting, I would gather leaves and branches for crafts or pick fruits for homemade jam.

During afternoon tea, Max would savour a cup of freshly brewed coffee accompanied by his homemade lemon cheesecake, while I would enjoy a cup of rose tea. We would watch the nearby sheep grazing, feeling a sense of divine comfort as if God Himself were our shepherd. In the evenings, Max and I would walk the dogs and return home under the twilight sky.

Reflecting on my childhood, playing on the grass with my younger brothers, rolling on the ground, and feeling unadulterated happiness fills me with warmth. Grandpa would play football with us while holding our baby sister, and our early years were profoundly intertwined with nature.

Ants, bugs, worms, and bees were part of our daily lives; they were never frightening but rather curious companions. Occasionally, in our playful enthusiasm, we might have inadvertently harmed them, but our fascination with nature was a constant. I am deeply grateful for those formative experiences, which allowed me to cherish the natural world from a young age. Reflecting on those times, I feel truly blessed.

Celebration

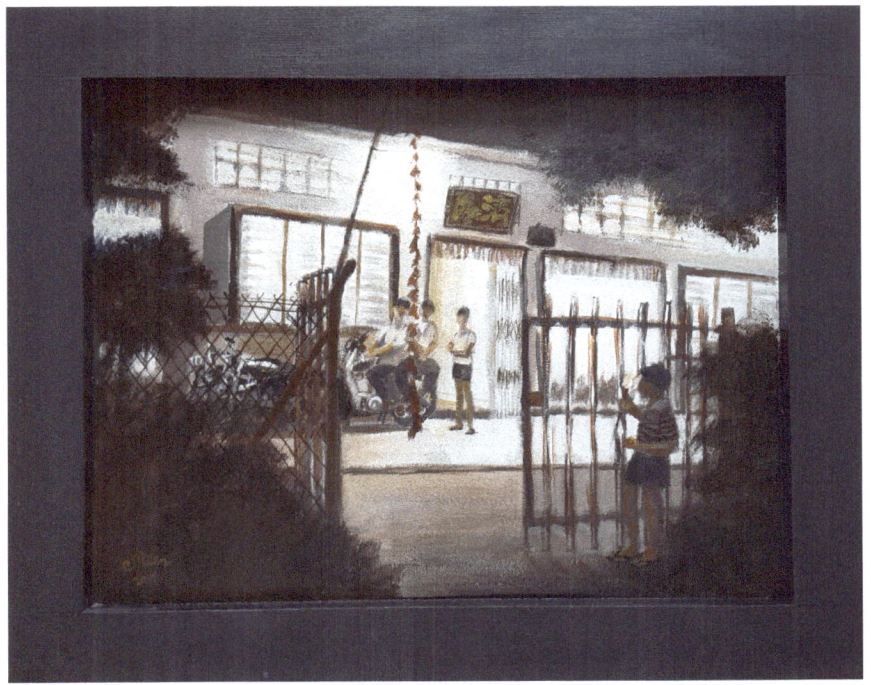

Acrylic on wooden board 53x43cm

Having been away from my hometown for many years, this painting evokes a poignant nostalgia, transporting me to a New Year's Eve from my secondary school years. It vividly captures the essence of

Chinese New Year in my Malaysian hometown.

I recall our family reunion dinners with great fondness, where laughter and stories flowed as freely as the food. After the meal, my brothers and cousins would set off long strings of firecrackers. The warmth of those memories envelops me like a treasured old sweater.

In the painting, my courageous little cousin, holding a lit incense stick, stands ready to ignite the firecrackers from the iron gate. The air is thick with anticipation as other cousins gather around, their faces illuminated with excitement.

Over the years, our celebrations have evolved, but the joy of witnessing fireworks illuminating the midnight sky has remained constant. Together, we marvelled at the brilliant colours, our laughter blending with the display.

Chinese New Year was always a time for our family to unite in abundance and togetherness. Our home would be adorned with vibrant lanterns and decorations, the aroma of traditional dishes filling the air. Leaving some food uneaten was a hopeful promise of prosperity.

At midnight, my mother would offer pastries to the God of Wealth, placing them on a table in the front yard. We would then gather for New Year's tea, enjoying conversations and festive TV programs, savouring our togetherness. Children would indulge in card games, a special treat only during the first four days, with peanuts, sunflower seeds, and small change as stakes. Seeing my mother join in the game, her laughter harmonizing with ours, was a joy in itself. We stayed up all night on New Year's Eve, believing it would ensure longevity and good health for our parents.

The first day of the New Year was marked by special customs: no arguments, no sweeping or washing dishes to avoid sweeping away our good fortune. The absence of scolding made the celebration even more magical. While we may not cling to superstitions, we cherish the customs of mutual congratulations, auspicious greetings, and red envelopes—symbols of blessings for the year ahead.

We wore new clothes, visited relatives and friends with joyful greetings, and delighted in receiving red envelopes filled with money. It was my favourite time of the year, a welcome respite from school. My father prepared sumptuous meals, while my mother managed the cleaning, making the holiday even more enjoyable.

The streets came alive with dragon and lion dances, the vibrant performances creating an electrifying atmosphere. We would invite the lion dancers into our home, hoping their presence would usher in good luck and prosperity.

Chinese New Year is far more than a festival; it reaffirms our bonds, a time when we come together to share in the blessings of family and wish for the best in the year ahead.

Connection

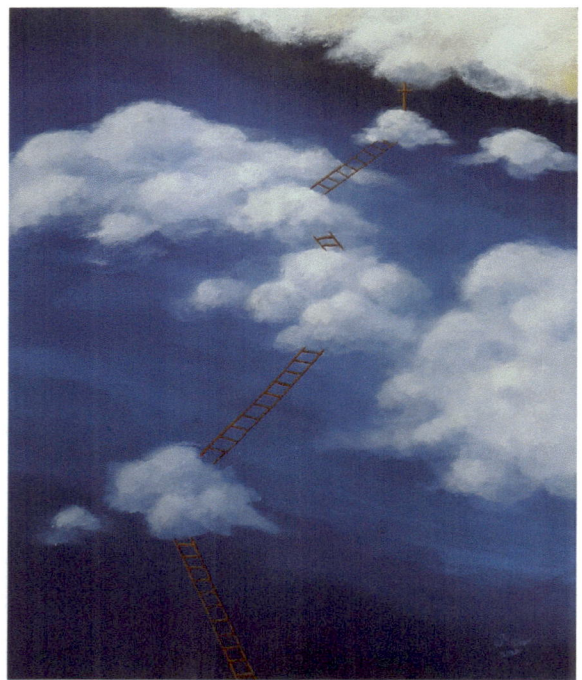

Acrylic on canvas 50x60cm

T wo years ago, while participating in an art fellowship in London, I was given the responsibility of designing and curating an exhibition. It was an intense and demanding time, and I completed this particular painting just two days before the exhibition's opening. Initially, the piece depicted a vibrant scene, a large shoal of fish swimming in the sea. Yet, as I signed my name, I felt a lingering sense of dissatisfaction, as if something essential was missing.

In a moment of quiet reflection, a new vision suddenly filled my mind: a vast sea of clouds beneath a brilliant blue sky, where white clouds were connected by ladders. The highest cloud, radiant and expansive, bore only a cross, with no ladder leading to it. This cloud, seemingly embodying heaven itself, inspired me to capture this vision on canvas. Though I had no spare canvas, I felt compelled to paint over the fish, embracing this new inspiration with a bold sense of purpose.

As I painted, I began to contemplate my own life. I realized that I had always relied on self-reliance and hard work, believing these were the keys to success. I had never placed my faith in a higher power, instead depending solely on my own efforts. I strove to be a good person, a diligent student, a dutiful child, and a dedicated employee, convinced that my actions alone would lead me to happiness and fulfilment, much like the ladders in my painting reaching toward the heavens.

Yet, despite my best efforts, true happiness remained elusive. I came to understand that genuine joy and peace stem from living a meaningful life and possessing a contented heart. Eventually, I came to know God and grasped the true essence of eternal life. The ladders in my painting evolved into a powerful metaphor for my spiritual journey: no matter how high I climbed, without knowing God, I could not reach heaven. The Bible teaches that only through Jesus's salvation and His cross, the ultimate path, can we reconcile with God and return to Him. This profound realization touched me deeply: heaven is God's home, and without a relationship with Him, how could He welcome us? Only by becoming His children can we enter the home He has prepared for us, heaven.

Looking back, I now understand that self-reliance alone could never satisfy my deepest yearnings or bring true fulfilment. True happiness, joy, and peace come from God, whose peace surpasses anything the world can offer. God's teachings guide us to love our enemies, to love selflessly, to be considerate, to respect others, to seek peace, and to treat people with kindness. These principles transformed my perspective and revealed life's true purpose.

In my painting, the ladders ascending to the final cloud symbolize our efforts and aspirations. Yet, without the cross, which symbolizes Jesus's sacrifice and resurrection, we cannot reach heaven. The cross replaces the ladder, offering redemption and access, not through our own efforts, but through the forgiveness of our sins. Confession and forgiveness restore our relationship with God, reconnecting us with Him for eternity.

Green Paradise

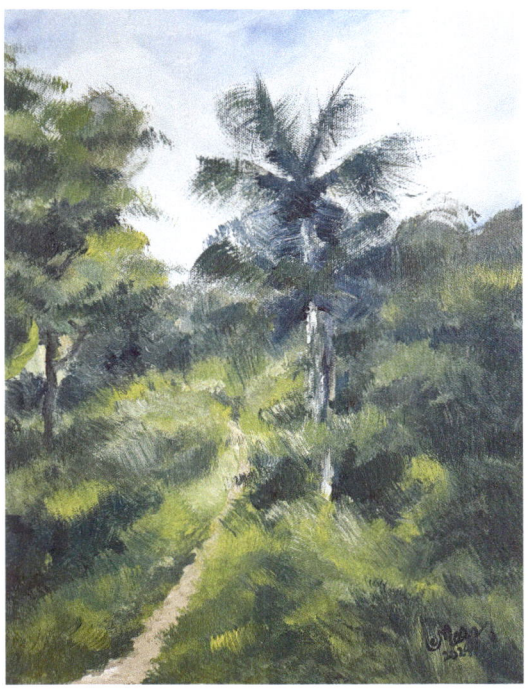

Acrylic on canvas 30x40cm

D uring a visit to Malaysia, I joined a friend on a site visit to Bentong, a town known for its ginger and tropical fruits. Among its treasures is the durian, a fruit with a reputation for its potent aroma and custard-like texture. The rolling hills, lush durian trees, and vibrant greenery captured my heart. Inspired by this enchanting landscape, I felt compelled to immortalize its beauty on canvas, hoping to convey the divine splendour of this verdant paradise.

That afternoon is etched vividly in my memory. The sun blazed with a golden intensity, casting a warm glow. When we arrived at the durian orchard, it was nestled within a tapestry of rolling hills and valleys. Before us, a vibrant jungle unfolded, filled with trees, under brush, and wildflowers. Coconut and papaya trees mingled with the towering durian trees, creating a rich mosaic of nature.

Accompanied by a few friendly dogs, we began our hike. Despite the occasional buzz of mosquitoes, our repellent kept them at bay, allowing us to savour the fresh, untainted air — a welcome escape from the city's clamour. Each breath felt like a cleansing, leaving us invigorated and deeply refreshed.

The hike was both exhilarating and serene. When we reached the summit, the view took my breath away. The endless sea of green stretched before us, like a living painting crafted by time itself. We collected a few pieces of weathered wood along the way, intending to turn them into keepsakes to forever remind us of this moment.

Our descent was slower, weighed down by the wood we carried. The dogs, ever faithful, led the way, pausing to make sure we followed. We stopped frequently to photograph the tranquil scenery, each shot a tribute to the untouched beauty surrounding us. This journey was a revelation, a reminder of the importance of preserving such serene landscapes from the advance of modernity. It was clear to me that this land should remain a sanctuary, a heaven for wildlife and natural beauty.

I am filled with a deep hope that this exquisite place will always be protected. It stands as a testament to nature's purest form, deserving our utmost care against the pressures of urban expansion. As I left, I carried with me not just photographs but a renewed sense of awe and gratitude for the natural world. My wish is that these breathtaking landscapes retain their untouched beauty, honouring the divine artistry that shaped them.

In the Park

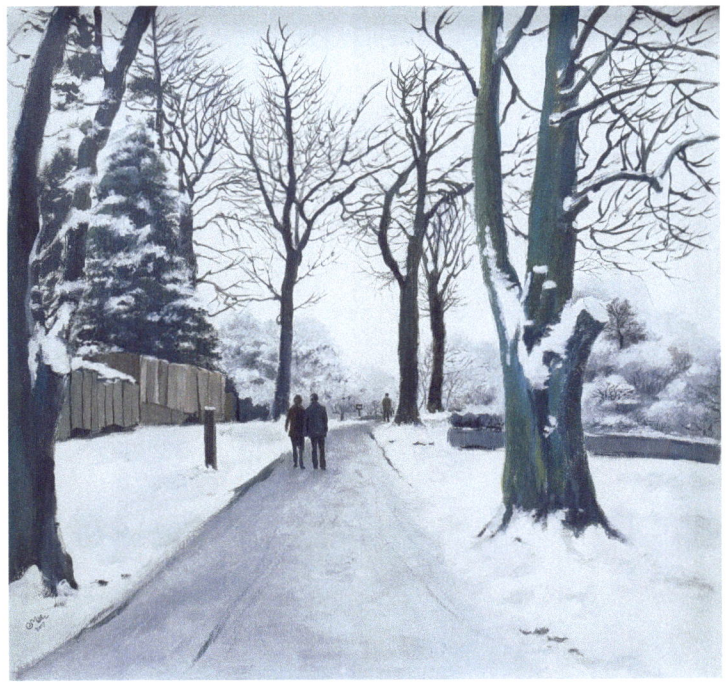

Acrylic on wooden board 71x70cm

For eight and a half years, we have been fortunate to share a home with a wonderful family in a spacious seven-room house. Our bedroom, facing east, offers a view of their lush backyard. From our window, we can see the trees and catch a glimpse of Golders Hill Park, a mere five-minute walk away. Almost every evening, Max and I take a leisurely stroll through the park, hand in hand, leaving behind a trail of countless footprints.

Near the park entrance, just beyond the tennis courts and accessible via a charming, winding path, lies a delightful little zoo. This enchanting haven, home to gentle animals, exudes a serene and joyful ambiance. Beyond the zoo, a picturesque bridge arches gracefully over a stream, leading to the children's playground: a vibrant space perpetually alive with the laughter and enthusiasm of children.

Another cherished spot in the park is a cosy café situated on a gentle hill near a different entrance. On weekends, Max and I often visit for a romantic brunch. The café's small, delicious buns are both delightful and affordable. We always choose a booth overlooking the park's lush green lawn, where we can bask in the tranquil view and occasionally glimpse the neighbouring town.

The park's beauty endures throughout the year, with vibrant flowers, lush plants, and majestic trees gracing every season. Near the café, a meticulously maintained flowerbed showcases the gardeners' seasonal efforts, offering a continually fresh and colourful display. Adjacent to this flowerbed is a serene lake, where ducks, geese, and occasional pigeons frolic. The birds' cheerful sounds and playful antics add a charming touch to the park's romantic allure.

One particularly unforgettable scene occurred during a winter more than a decade ago. An extraordinary snowfall had blanketed the city, transforming it into a magical winter wonderland. The snowstorm brought all transportation to a standstill until the following day. Seizing this rare opportunity, we ventured to the park. At the entrance, we observed a couple walking hand in hand, their tender footprints delicately etched in the snow as they entered. I endeavoured to capture this poignant moment on canvas; their gentle and enduring presence profoundly moved us. It was a heart-warming reminder of our own aspiration to grow old together, hand in hand, as they had.

Inside the park, the snow-covered slopes became a joyous playground. Families skied, engaged in playful snowball fights, and built whimsical snowmen with their children. The tree trunks and branches, draped in snow, contributed to the pristine, white landscape. Everything appeared strikingly clean and pure. We took many beautiful photographs, though we did not linger long in the park.

Golders Hill Park, with its lively scenes and many cosy moments, holds a special place in our lives. It serves as a serene sanctuary where we can relax, reflect, and connect with nature and each other. It is a haven where we create lasting memories and dream of our future.

Journey Home

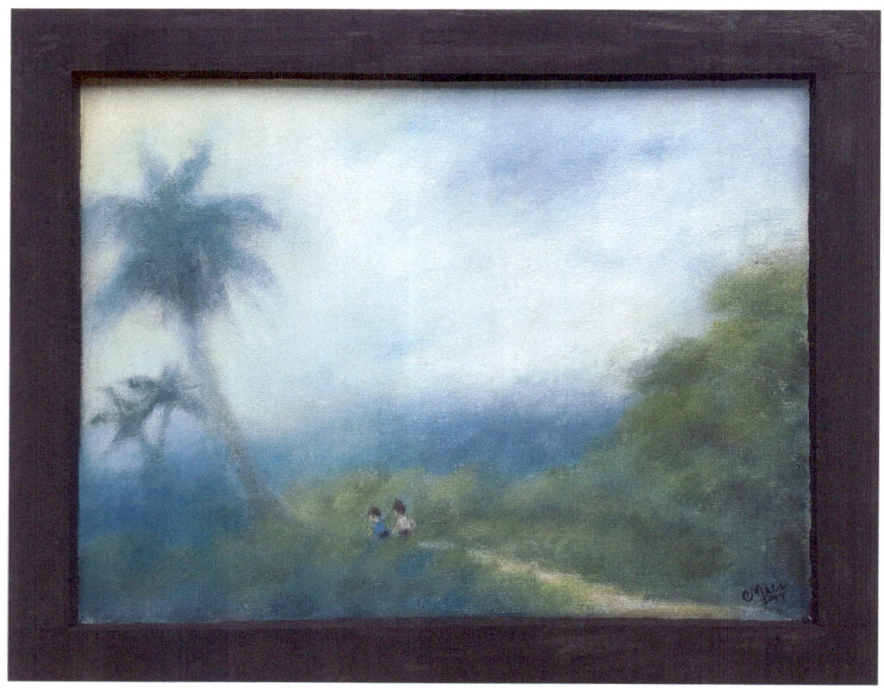

Acrylic on wooden board 50x40cm

As a child, life in our small wooden house with two bedrooms and a living room was both modest and bustling. Mum and Dad occupied one room, while us five siblings shared the other. Our home relied on a well out front, as running water was a luxury we didn't have; the entire village depended on these wells for their daily needs.

A red dirt road bordered the left side of our house, leading to a marshy area with a small pond just beyond it. Adjacent to the pond was our neighbour's pigsty, home to over a dozen pigs. The pond itself was a sanctuary for us; we spent hours catching small fish and soaking our feet in its cool, refreshing water. The area was a lush tapestry of dense weeds and various trees, including coconut, papaya, cassava, sweet potatoes, and banana trees, planted by our neighbours. The foliage buzzed with life, from insects to snakes, monkeys, and squirrels.

We revealed in chasing butterflies through the grass and playing hide-and-seek with the neighbourhood kids, our imaginations turning every corner into a grand adventure.

Insects were our constant companions. We caught spiders and kept them in matchboxes, staging races with those caught by other children. Tying threads to dragonflies, we watched them dance in the air, chasing after them with delight. We crafted wooden guns from branches, creating bullets from plant seeds tied to rubber bands. We competed with neighbourhood kids to shoot down tin cans, each competition a joyous blur of laughter, with the gentle breeze playing with our hair and the warm sunlight kissing our faces.

Learning to ride bicycles added another layer of excitement; we raced each other, occasionally falling and earning scrapes and bruises, only to be gently scolded by our parents afterward.

Flying kites was another cherished pastime. We made kites in various shapes, such as birds, eagles, and butterflies, using bamboo and paper. Watching them soar against the backdrop of a deep blue sky filled our hearts with pure happiness.

As the sun set each evening, casting a warm glow of orange and pink across the sky, we reluctantly made our way home. The marsh, pond, and surrounding bushes were not just our playground; they were a world of magic and exploration, offering new discoveries and unforgettable memories each day.

This painting captures the joyous scene of my younger brothers playing in the jungle all day as we happily made our way home for dinner one evening. These simple joys of rural life are etched in our hearts forever, a testament to the beauty of our childhood adventures.

Midnight in Paris

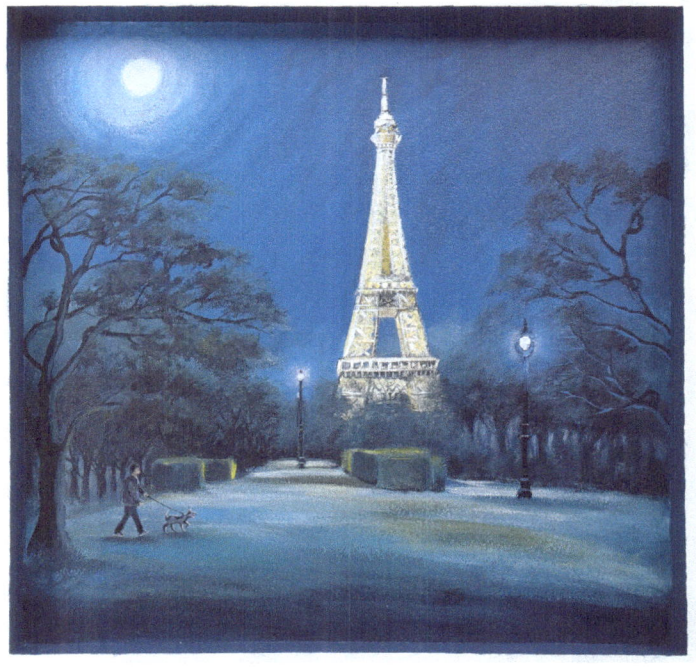

Acrylic on wooden board 71x70cm

I have often imagined living romantically with Max in Paris. In my dream, Max falls in love with the city during a trip and decides to stay. Unlike him, I came to Paris to study art and remained, enduring numerous hardships, which I humorously refer to as "artistic sacrifices."

We met and fell in love in this romantic city, residing in a charming apartment near the Eiffel Tower. From there, we could gaze upon the iconic structure in the distance, watching as it gradually blends into the twilight at sunset. Standing tall by the River Seine, it transforms into a vision of elegance, like a beautiful woman who works tirelessly during the day and dons a sparkling evening gown at night, occasionally dazzling with golden light as she joyfully prepares for a romantic evening.

After dinner, Max and I would indulge in a classic French film, and afterward, stroll hand in hand under the soft glow of moonlight near the Eiffel Tower, which stands as a silent sentinel in the night sky until dawn heralds a new day.

Max loves to take his loyal dog, Mountain, for midnight walks along the serene streets near the Eiffel Tower. Mountain's long nails make a rhythmic clicking sound, clear and crisp on the quiet cobblestones of Paris. As they pass by trees, Mountain marks his territory, perhaps fearing that Max might wander too far and lose his way. Under the watchful gaze of the Eiffel Tower, Max and Mountain continue their midnight promenades through Paris, passing quiet cafes and charming little shops.

Several months ago, on a sudden impulse, I flew to Paris with another artist friend. We attended a mesmerizing exhibition of Mark Rothko, the acclaimed American abstract painter, and visited the vibrant artists' studios and galleries at 59 Rivoli.

The story of 59 Rivoli is particularly inspiring. In 1999, three daring artists illegally occupied this building, abandoned by a bank and the state since 1989, in the heart of Paris, to live and create. When the French government sued them for eviction in 2000, they garnered significant media attention and support. Eventually, in 2001, the city of Paris purchased the building and officially designated it as studios for these artists. Now, a total of 31 artists create and exhibit their works at 59 Rivoli.

These artists reignited a nearly forgotten dream of mine. Now, we live in London, just a few hours by train from Paris, and have only visited Paris twice. Is there a chance for us to fulfil my long-held dream of living in Paris for a while? Even just a few months would be satisfying.

And so, I painted the story of my dream of Paris, hoping it will one day come true. The painting, titled "Midnight in Paris," draws inspiration from a film of the same name with its enchanting romance. The protagonist finds himself travelling through time, encountering luminaries like Ernest Hemingway, Pablo Picasso, and Salvador Dalí in the same tavern. As he shifts between past and present, he ultimately meets his dream girl by the River Seine and falls in love at first sight, much like my own deep affection for Paris.

Little Pond

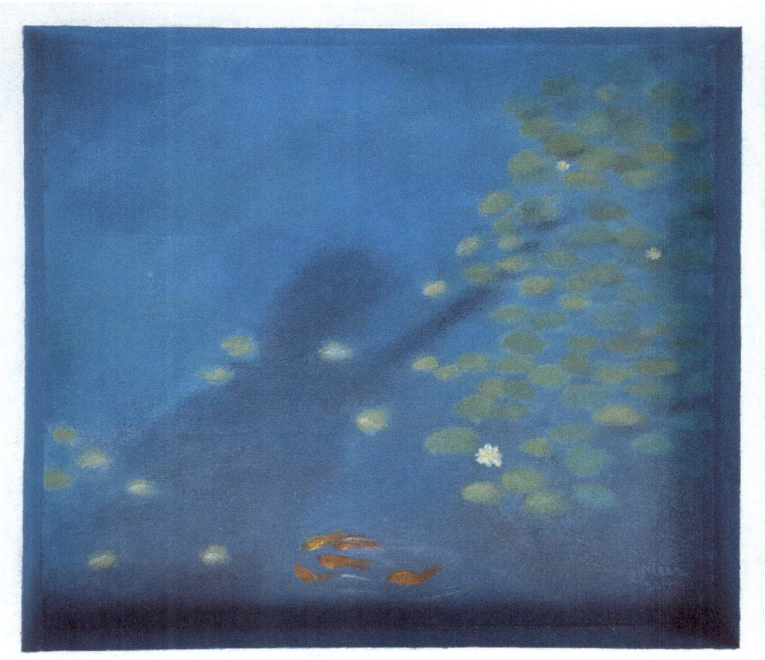

Acrylic on wooden board 44x40cm

I n the southern part of a small village, our wooden house stood resolutely across a muddy road from a landscape enveloped by dense bushes, swamps, and ponds. This rustic setting, where nature flourished in its raw beauty, became the backdrop of my childhood and the inspiration for my painting. With my two brothers, two sisters, and our neighbourhood friends, we immersed ourselves in endless adventures, exploring every corner of our natural playground.

The village, adorned with tall coconut trees, papaya trees, banana trees, and fields of cassava and sweet potatoes, was a canvas of simple fun and discovery. Each day after school, we eagerly embarked on our daily escapades. Near a little pond, our neighbour's pig farm bustled with life. The pigs, contentedly munching on water hyacinth plants and wallowing in the mud, created a symphony of grunts and snorts that became a familiar and comforting soundtrack to our childhood.

One of our favourite pastimes was catching dragonflies. Armed with sticks made from coconut leaves tipped with sticky latex, we carefully captured the colourful insects, admiring their delicate wings before releasing them back into the wild. The act of catching and releasing these vibrant creatures became a cherished ritual, a moment of connection with the intricate beauty of nature.

Another treasured activity was catching tadpoles, which we kept in glass bottles and watched with fascination as they grew and transformed. The little pond near our house was a beloved spot where we also caught tiny fish in the stream, bringing them home in glass bottles to marvel at their shimmering, glimmering bodies. These simple acts of exploration and wonder formed the essence of our daily lives.

Hide and seek among the thick bushes was a daily game, the thrill of hiding and being found never losing its allure. Our adventures occasionally brought unexpected encounters, like stumbling upon a snake, which sent us screaming and running in a flurry of excitement and fear. Monkeys, too, roamed the area, their chatter and acrobatics adding a wild, almost magical dimension to our playground.

In this picturesque village, every day was a new chapter in the never-ending story of our childhood. This painting captures the essence of that time, a testament to the simple, profound beauty of nature and the boundless joy of youthful adventure. Through each brushstroke, I aim to relive those moments and share the enchanting world we once inhabited, where the wonders of nature and the innocence of youth intertwined in perfect harmony.

Meet me at sunset

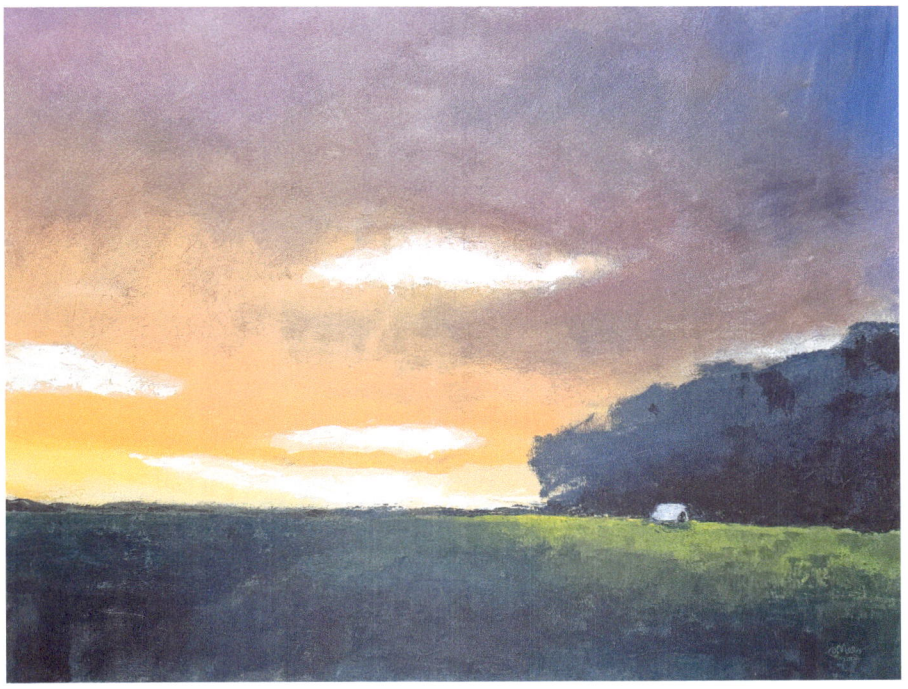

Acrylic on canvas 80x100cm

During my primary school years, our form teacher often encouraged us to recite poetry, infusing the beauty of classical literature into our daily routines. I vividly recall one lesson where we recited a

Tang Dynasty poem titled ""). The verses spoke of the sunset's breathtaking beauty, even as dusk approached: "The sunset is infinitely beautiful, but it is near dusk." Our teacher explained that this imagery of the setting sun, with its fleeting splendour fading into twilight, symbolized the transitory nature of beautiful moments. He urged us to treasure the present, for time passes swiftly. At that time, my teacher was in the prime of his life. Yet, when we reunited years later, both of us had greyed with the passage of time.

Inspired by such reflections, I have painted countless sunset scenes. After school, I often walked home at sunset, the sky transitioning from bright hues to the encroaching darkness of dusk. Those were hurried, youthful steps as we scurried home before nightfall. As I grew older, a song titled "Walking Home at Sunset" gained popularity, its cheerful rhythm and rustic melody mirroring the very scenes I sought to capture on canvas.

In this painting lies a story of my imagination — a vision of myself in a vast green field as the sun begins its descent, bathing everything in a warm, golden light. The air is rich with the fragrance of wildflowers, and the small town grows tranquil as night approaches. The windows of wooden houses on the prairie start to glow softly, while distant laughter mingles with the encroaching darkness.

I remember a promise made under a sunset many years ago:

"I will return to see you, the sunset, and this prairie in three years." I can still recall the warmth of your hand in mine and the tear that shimmered in your eye, reflecting the setting sun. That was the last time we saw each other before you departed, leaving quietly two days later, journeying to a distant place without me.

As the sky deepened into shades of orange and pink, I gathered my thoughts of longing and picked a bunch of yellow wildflowers. With twilight settling in, I retraced my steps. The night gently enveloped the land, and a soft breeze brushed across the grass, carrying the echoes of our past conversations. Birds chirped as they returned to their nests, and the town's evening sounds waned as everyone retreated home. I could almost see your familiar figure waiting in front of the wooden house, hoping for my return.

My yearning for you lingers like the scent of summer flowers carried by the wind, persistent and intertwined with the aroma of sun-dried clothes. As the last ray of sunlight yielded to dusk, I found solace in the promise of two years hence.

We would meet again in this verdant field, stroll along the paths between the fields, and share tales of our lives since we parted. The little house would await us as we chased the sunset, walking home at dusk, with the promise of creating new memories under the golden light.

See You Again

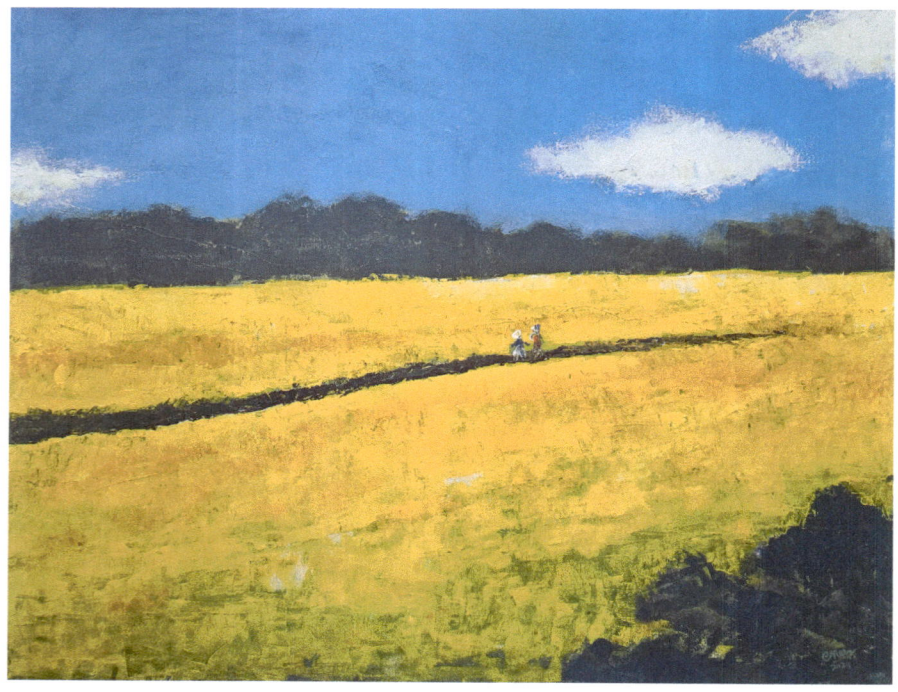

Acrylic on canvas 80x100cm

I can't remember exactly when my affection for flowers began or when I first became fascinated by the art of growing them. Yet, I have a vivid memory from my secondary school days that marks my first significant flower-planting adventure. I took on the task of clearing the weeds in front of our old home, working the soil with a hoe until it was loose and ready. I planted a sprawling patch of marigolds, embarking on my first major floral project.

The marigolds flourished with minimal effort, requiring only daily watering. Soon, the garden was a riot of vibrant blooms, so dazzlingly bright they were nearly blinding. Despite their strong scent, sometimes derisively called "chicken poop flowers" by those less enamoured, the marigolds' robust growth caught everyone's attention.

Neighbors frequently stopped to chat as I tended to the flowers in the evening. Flower enthusiasts would ask for seeds, and before long, every household on the street had embraced the beauty of gardening. This collective effort transformed our street into a stunning tapestry of colour.

I still remember the first time I saw the marigolds in full bloom. It was a sunny day, with a gentle breeze, and the golden flowers sparkled under the sunlight. In that moment, I felt a profound sense of accomplishment and joy, as though each flower was smiling at me, thanking me for my care. That experience ignited a deep love for growing flowers and left me with cherished memories.

Later, as I left home for school, my opportunities to plant flowers diminished. Those days became fond recollections. In my dreams, I often return to that sea of yellow, inhaling the familiar fragrance and basking in the warmth of those simpler times. These dreams bring me comfort and nostalgia, a yearning for the carefree days of my youth.

After graduation, I returned home and was delighted to find that the street was still adorned with a vibrant array of flowers. My neighbours had continued, with even greater enthusiasm, the floral tradition that I had started. Seeing this filled me with immense satisfaction, knowing that my small gesture had inspired a community-wide passion for gardening.

The painting I created represents these memories. It depicts a golden expanse, intentionally abstract to invite personal interpretation. Whether you see sunflowers, chive blossoms, or even marigolds, the painting allows for your imagination to take flight.

In the painting, you see the past and present versions of me meeting in the flower field, upholding our annual promise. Each blooming season, we reunite in this radiant space, savouring the summer days and cherishing our time together until the sunset. We eagerly anticipate the same day each year to reconnect.

As time goes by and I grow older, our promise remains steadfast. Each flower season, we return to this cherished field, celebrating both past and present. Though the world around us changes and time marches on, the flower field endures, its blossoms ever vibrant.

One particularly hot year, the flowers bloomed earlier than usual. As always, we met amidst the floral expanse, strolling together and reflecting on our youthful dreams and present lives. Under the bright blue sky and white clouds, with the sun casting its warm glow over the flower field, we walked hand in hand. The field shimmered in the afternoon light, and we were enveloped in a profound sense of joy and contentment.

This painting is not just a portrayal of memories but a testament to future hopes. No matter how time evolves, the flower field, the flowers, and our annual meetings will remain a constant, walking an eternal path together.

The Sea and Me

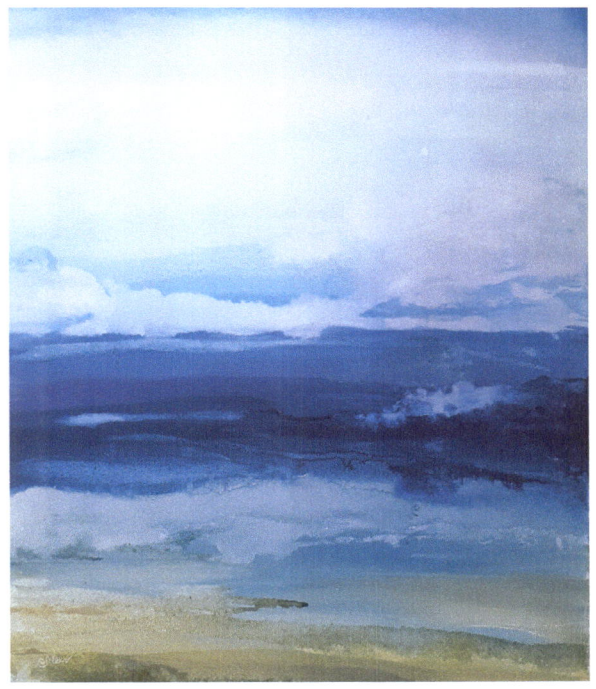

Acrylic on canvas 50x60cm

U pon moving to London, I was struck by a sudden longing for the fresh seafood I had once taken for granted. The distance from the bright blue sea, the soft sandy beaches, and the delightful seafood of my childhood deepened my sense of displacement.

This painting reflects my profound longing for the sea of my hometown. Inspired by vivid memories and the tranquil beach near Kuantan, Malaysia, it captures the beauty and serenity of that cherished place. The pristine white sands of the beach surpass even the hues rendered in this painting. I fondly remember a night spent at a seaside hotel during our honeymoon in 1995, a moment forever etched in my heart.

The boundless ocean, with its deep blue waters and the rhythmic symphony of waves against the shore, has always been a sanctuary of comfort for me. I miss the gentle sea breeze and the fine, white sand that invited me to rest. I remember running barefoot along the beach, feeling the soft, yielding sand beneath my feet, and watching my footprints dissolve as the waves tenderly erased them.

From an early age, I dreamed of living by the sea. I envisioned starting each day with a swim in the ocean and savouring a simple breakfast with a view of the water, seagulls soaring above.

Yet, my childhood home was nestled at the base of a mountain, far from the sea and rivers. The climate was often stifling, with unpredictable showers drenching clothes left out to dry.

Fortunately, a seaside town lay about ten miles from my home. Occasionally, I would take a bus there to experience the sea, watch the sunset, and listen to the evening chorus of birds returning to their nests. Despite the occasional clamour, these visits brought me immense joy.

Later, I was transferred to a high school in that seaside town, commuting daily for two years. Each morning, a student bus would take me and my classmates on a bumpy, ten-mile ride. Though we departed early, delays were common as the bus avoided the coastal route, depriving me of glimpses of the sea. My daily commute, which consumed two to three hours, became more manageable when I moved closer to the school in my second year, sharing a room with four classmates to save time for studying.

In the afternoons, when the sun's intensity waned, I would bike to an old tree by a large grassy field near the sea. There, I would immerse myself in reading while enjoying the sea breeze. I recall one day being so absorbed in my book that I failed to notice ant bites on my toes. Upon inspection, I discovered a nest at the tree's roots, likely disturbed by my presence.

Evenings in the seaside town were lively. The grassy fields were filled with people running, playing, and socializing. A local named Max often played football there, and he might have seen a young girl engrossed in her books beneath the old tree. Perhaps our paths crossed without our knowledge, missing a chance to connect. Many years later, fate reunited us elsewhere, and Max and I eventually married.

When I needed a respite from my reading, I would visit the beach to feel the sea breeze tousling my hair. I would buy a bowl of mixed fruit and vegetable "Rojak" from a nearby stall, savouring it while listening to the sea's rhythmic sounds and watching the waves dance. The sea, in its perpetual motion, surged with intensity at times and flowed gently at others. It extended to the turtle-shaped island on the horizon, and occasionally, a distant grey-black ship would pass slowly. The sea's vast presence provided solace, offering a temporary escape from the stress of exams.

The rhythm of the sea felt like a vital force of life, renewing the earth and maintaining the balance of the global ecosystem. In its quiet moments, I sensed a heartbeat, a rhythm that connected it to all living things.

As the sun set, casting an orange-red glow over the sea, I would ride my bike home in the twilight. A few young people would linger on the grassy field, resting and chatting after their football game, as the sun's afterglow slowly faded, signalling the end of another day.

Conclusion

This book has been a deeply personal journey, reflecting the stories and emotions woven into my paintings. Each piece is a testament to how art can convey profound narratives. I hope you uncover the stories behind the brushstrokes and find a personal connection as you explore them. Creating this book has been a labour of love, fuelled by my passion for storytelling through art.

Afterword

Reflecting on the past seven years, a period marked by profound farewells and the unprecedented trials of a global pandemic, I found myself on the brink of despair. Yet, amid this upheaval, an unexpected opportunity for a fresh start emerged. I took up my pen once again and embarked on a new journey of painting and writing.

My deepest gratitude goes to my parents in heaven, Max, family, and friends. Thank you for standing by me and sharing in this adventure.

This book, The Stories in Paintings, fulfils my mother's dream and serves as a tribute to her. I hope that within these pages, you find a subtle resonance and that it sparks a small flame in your heart, just as it has in mine.

I would be delighted to hear your reflections and thoughts about this book. Your feedback means the world to me.

The Artist-Author
Mee Mee Chai

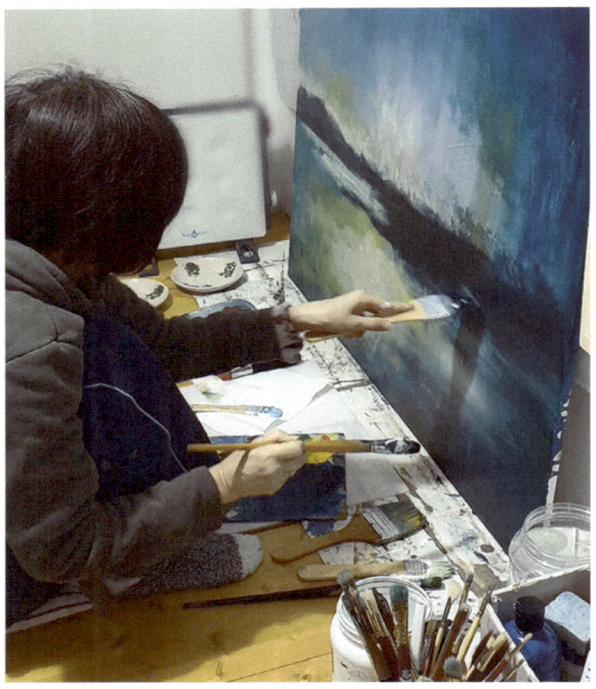

The artist-author Mee Mee creating moments in her little studio

Mee Mee Chai, also known as Miuko "美雨子", is a London-based versatile artist and writer originally from Malaysia. She paints, writes, and designs, with her creative journey shaped by a background in commercial art and interior design. This diverse experience enables her to bring artistic visions to life across various mediums, including wood, canvas, and paper.

In addition to her visual art, Mee Mee co-authored *Handwritten*, sharing heartfelt reflections on life and writing. She has held diverse roles such as production coordinator, interior designer, lecturer, journalist, editor, and columnist. Her work resonates with audiences and is collected globally.

Mee Mee's unique style reflects her deep appreciation for creation's beauty, inviting viewers to immerse themselves in the narrative of each piece. Her art offers a meaningful connection to the rich stories and emotions embedded in her work.

AFTERWORD

Social media links

Web > meemeechai.com

Facebook > meemeechai

Instagram > @meemee.chai

www.ingramcontent.com/pod-product-compliance
Lightning Source LLC
Chambersburg PA
CBHW040332220526
45473CB00009B/2652